Wolf Moon Down

Sarah J. Woolf-Wade

Goose River Press
Waldoboro, Maine

Copyright © 2018 Sarah J. Woolf-Wade

All rights reserved. With the exception of quotations drawn from classical sources, no part of this book may be reproduced or transmitted in any form without permission from the publisher.

Library of Congress Control Card Number: 2018908348.

ISBN: 978-1-59713-197-1

First Printing, 2018

Cover Art: *Moon Reach* by Sally Loughridge, soft pastel on panel, 20 x 20."

Published by
Goose River Press
3400 Friendship Road
Waldoboro, Maine 05472
www.gooseriverpress.com

Native Americans' Full Moon names were created to help different tribes track the seasons. The Colonial Americans adopted most of them. Each full moon name came from the Algonquin tribes who lived in regions from New England to Lake Superior. Each full moon name was applied to the entire month in which it occurred. The Wolf Moon appeared in January, when wolves howled in hunger outside the villages.

Acknowledgments

In appreciation to editors of the following publications in which versions of these poems first appeared.

Animus: "Lady on the Boat with Flowers" and "Nightsong"

Down the Bristol Road: "Northhaven Autumn"

Frost Place Anthology: "Dropped Stitches"

Goose River Anthology: "Depending on the Tide," "Minstrel," "Flood Waters," and "Deadly Conflict"

Midcoast Audubon Bulletin: "The Forest Circle"

Oberon Poetry Magazine: "Inisheer Sweater"

Port City Poems: "Deadly Conflict"

Puckerbrush Review: "Slack Water"

Seasons of the Soul: "Winter Ghazal"

Stanza (Maine Poets Society) : "The House Comes Down," and "No Man's Land"

Take Heart (Maine Anthology): "Making the Turn"

The Watershed: "Loon Alone"

My thanks to the poets for their years of guidance at the Frost Place and the Key West Literary Seminar. Appreciation is given to the Maine Poets Society for a grant to study at the Palm Beach Poetry Festival. My gratitude for artistic advice from poets Dona Stein, Anne Mullin, George Van Deventer, and editor Deborah J. Benner. Special gratitude is offered to Nancy Adams for inestimable digital help, and to Stan Wade for his patience.

Table of Contents

Bays, Islands, and Other Shores

Winter Moonset//1
Chartless//2
Fear of Drowning//3
Geese on a Mirror//4
Burnt Island Secret//5
After the Concert, Monhegan Island//6
Island School Dooryard//7
Slow Down//8
Lady on the Boat with Flowers//10
No Man's Land//11
Northhaven Autumn, a sonnet//12
Slack Water//13
Tidepools//14
Loon Alone//15
Nightsong//16

Home Is the Sailor

Swimming Upstream//19
Considering Exodus//20
I'm Staying//21
Defiant//22
My Father Lives Here//23
Reflection//24
Internal Correspondence//25
Where Does it Come From?//26

Table of Contents

Alice in Technoland//27
Dropped Stitches//28
Message//30
Land-Locked//31

Changing Landscapes

The Old Garden Remains//35
The House Comes Down//36
Flood Waters//37
Two Trees//38
The Brook//39
Nothing on Earth Is Meant to Stay//40

Far, Far Away

Sleeping Under Mosquito Netting//43
Lago Maggiore//45
The Biggest and Most Silent//46
Iceberg, St. Anthony's Harbor, Newfoundland//48
The Shattered Balkans//50
The Boys of Orkney//51
An Old Woman's Farewell to St. Kilda//52
Duval Street, Key West//54
Boundaries//56
Inisheer Sweater//57
The Swimming Sleeper//58

Table of Contents

Good People, Old and Young

Light in the Window//61
Two Young Mothers with Babies//62
Deadly Conflict//64
Jane Austin's Girls//65
Eventful Day in an Edwardian Family//67
Outbound Alone//68
Unfinished Gardener//69
Summer in Miami//70
Banjo//71
Good Old Men//72
School Reunion//73
Photograph of Innocence//74
Hide and Seek//75
Boys at the Back of the Bus//77
Fishing in the Rain//78
First Encounter, A METCO Child Meets the Ocean//79
Winter Recess Lament//81

Darkness and Nightmares

Dreams Haiku//85
Phantom Boatman//86
Writer's Nightmare//87
Ascending a Maze to Escape//88
Letting Go//89
Denouement//90

Table of Contents

Dark Island//91
Reruns//92

Maine Winter and Other Seasons

Making the Turn//95
October Wind and Daylight Savings Time (Haikus)//96
New Season//97
Winter Solstice//98
Rise of Coastal Water//99
Mornings Below Zero//100
Winter Warfare//101
Winter Ghazal//102
Winter Work//103
Mud Season Advice//104
Spring Burst//105
The Sounds of Silence//106

Aging and Ending

Depending on the Tide//109
Barter//110
Radiation//111
Waiting for an Answer//112
Youth Scramble//113
Another New Day//115
Too Old//116
It's That Time//117

Table of Contents

Safekeeping//119
Colors Before Dark//120
Adrift in the Grass//121
Minstrel//122
Footsteps in the Night//123
How We Leave//124
The Forest Circle, a sonnet//125

Bays, Islands, and Other Shores

Winter Moonset

Wolf moon:
Full moon of January
gold in the heart of winter
sails across quivering water
to the black shore.
It lights a seductive path
cold over the bay
a bold invitation
in case I want to step outdoors
and follow.

Chartless

Drumlins
heave themselves up
from the depths of Penobscot Bay
like ghostly whales
surfacing for air.
Some are covered by spruces
ringed by welcoming sand,
others guarded by threatening cliffs.
Try to imagine Champlain
or other fearless explorers
four hundred years ago
navigating the shoals
not knowing the bottom
with only lead lines
to tell them the depths
like most of us, unwarned,
skimming heedless
over our surfaces
dangerously unaware
and unafraid
of what might lurk below.

Fear of Drowning

I yearned to be out on the water
and knew I had to do it myself.
My mate was out of sight all summer
but friends and I could cruise the bay
in *Pippi,* my secondhand runabout.

Down on the dock as I bailed out the dinghy,
panic engulfed me on the first day.
What if the motor failed, out on John's Bay?
Would the ebbtide drag me out to sea?
Could the current dash me up on the rocks?

If I fell overboard while alone in the boat
would I have enough strength to pull myself out?
As a child, I was a fairly strong swimmer
but now, alas, I am no longer young.
An aluminum boat can sink very fast.

I wondered what it must feel like to drown,
descend from the surface, run out of air,
bubbling water into my lungs.
Would I pass out in a timely fashion
and save someone the trouble of burial at sea?

The boat is still riding there, out on her mooring,
a single, tethered, lonely seabird.
She stands for freedom, but terror, as well.
You have to know enough to be scared
and a laugh is the other side of fear.

Geese on a Mirror

My eyes flashed over the bay
one cold March morning.
Two enormous Canada geese
floated on the still water
right on schedule,
a pair of feathery battleships
drifting on a watery mirror.

When I arose in a moment, they were gone
to join two more paddling farther north,
silent, mysterious, in ten-degree air,
faithful to their annual plan,
obedient to orbits of planets,
unaware that it was far
too soon for spring.

Burnt Island Secret

Moss, draped everywhere,
soft and wet underfoot,
hangs forlornly from branches,
climbs up and over dead bark.

A brave crabapple tree
stands sad and alone
near an ancient stone wall,
tumbling down from hill to shore.

Mist rises up from fog,
condenses on our eyelashes.
Sweat runs down our necks,
mixes cold with creeping rain.

Who tried to clear this stubborn land?
When did they abandon their homestead
on this unforgiving island?
Why did they leave it to rot in silence?

After the Concert
Monhegan Island

Quarter notes remaining from the Solstice Jamboree
hang suspended in raindrops
as I inch my way down the dark road
from the island church on the hill.

Tunes from fiddle and guitar
circle around my head
repetitively
with the underlying rhythm of the bass.

I remember
the miracle of a French horn
echoing the moan of the island foghorn
transformed into a mournful melody.

I shuffle carefully to avoid
potholes filled with standing water
rippling mirrors of fog
camouflaged pitfalls underfoot.

I regret the absence of flashlight
but no matter, scattered
helpful fireflies dance in the weeds
to light my way.

Island School Dooryard

Standing alone
in September sunshine
the one-room school may hum inside
but the dooryard is silent.
A single bicycle
is propped in the stand.
Beside it a liquid-eyed golden retriever
lies in the leftover summer grass
his wakeful head resting on paws.
In slow motion
he eases himself to his feet
ambles to the door
and stands watchful, waiting.
It is nearly noon.
He wonders if his young person
will come out for lunch soon
or maybe never again.

Slow Down

I must give myself
the gift of time
to see things clearly
without hurrying by.
It takes longer now
than many years ago,
to push myself
along the island trails.

I sit down on Burnt Head
my favorite rock above the cliffs
with meat and cheese,
strawberries and Merlot
to ease into the land
and admire the glittering sea.
Two chattering tourists
hurry to my perch.
"Is this Number One?"
they wonder, pointing to their map.
Before I can puzzle out an answer,
they blast onward,
galloping faster than they came.

I remember something
just like this, years ago
when there were deer
on Monhegan.
Two people charging ahead of me
on the trail
steamed on at high speed
to a destination—
who knows where?
They never caught a glimpse
of the big-eyed doe and her fawn
lying in the shade
by the side of the path
in the deep cool grass.

There is much to admire in the world
I've learned
if only we can slow down.

Lady on the Boat with Flowers

The October sea is rolling and
the *Laura B* backs away,
full power astern, then swings around.
On deck is a white-haired lady with flowers.

The summer waitstaff sailed out on an earlier boat
among friends waving wildly from the shore.
They scattered flowers over the rail
to ensure their island return some day.

Today the white-haired lady clutches flowers tight.
She holds Zinnias, Cosmos, Black-eyed Susans —
treasured gifts from someone's garden,
not pilfered from the island meadows.

She sways on deck with others who
hesitate to go below.
She lifts her hand and waves although
no one on shore returns her gesture.

Folks have trickled off the dock.
Trucks have lumbered up the hill.
Her flowers do not flutter over the side
There is no decent word for goodbye.

No Man's Land*

The rich build mansions on the shore.
They own the land and still want more.

They love the sound of ocean's growl
where ancient settlers fished and fowled.

They claim the sand above low tide,
they feel that they are justified

to stop our strolls along the beach
as far as surging waves can reach.

We disregard their power play
and track our age-old right of way.

We leave our footprints in the sand
above the tide in No Man's Land.

Cold waves that wet our feet are free.
No wealthy man can own the sea.

*No Man's Land: the space on the shore between mean high tide and mean low tide, historically free to all for use in navigation, fishing, and fowling. (Massachusetts and, ultimately, Maine law)

North Haven Autumn, a sonnet

At last the rusticating folks have gone.
The tennis nets are stored away somewhere.
No mowers hum along the sweeping lawns,
no sails drift down the empty Thorofare.

But lobster boats appear at morning light.
Old trucks emerge—no plates and worn-out treads.
Men check all doors and windows, sealed up tight.
No gardeners tend the faded flower beds.

The daily pace of living gradually slowed,
it's back to quilts and needles, hammers, nails,
to greeting friends on walks along the road,
to kitchen coffee laced with inside tales.

The tools and toys of summer stored on shelves,
the island families now have lives, themselves.

Slack Water

the sea breathes
neither in
nor out
but holds its breath
the current stops
our boat floats
on the still surface
balances on the lip of time
neither beginning
nor end
no water advances
or recedes
slack water

the Indians knew a place
called Oven's Mouth
in the river
where they could make
a passage
only at slack water
the past and future wait on either side
in one more minute
it will be too late
to make it

Tidepools

Tidepools
mirrors of the sky
scooped by giant hands
millions of years ago
miniature seas ringed by beards
quivering with tiny lives
like fish that swallow their young
rise and fall with the moon
in endless circular rhythm.
How many eyes now gone
have revealed themselves in the shallows?

Loon Alone

The loon has been single all through summer;
now autumn is creeping over the bay.
I am alone in the house at night
bent over the thirteenth draft of a poem
with doors and windows open to silence
when I hear the solitary call
plaintive, echoing over the water
yet no response from a mate nearby.
A solemn, hooting, sorrowful song,
an upturn at the end, like a question—
for me, this is the saddest sound.
I know the words as well as the singer;
many things don't go according to plan.

Nightsong

Seven lights bob in shivering night
Outside the mouth of John's Bay
Shrimp boats glimmer through watery darkness
Waiting for the nets to fill
Their lights, a glow of jewels
Sparkle on velvet skyline
Radio waves float their quiet voices
Signals leap across the blackness
Crackling with companionship
Aimless nighttime dreamlike words
Strung together by loneliness
Reaching out over wintry water
To touch some other men in boats
And listeners alone on shore
Eavesdroppers on the radio scanner
A fragile chain of reassurance
All holding hands in the dark

Home Is the Sailor

Swimming Upstream

I have come back
to the land of my conception
though not to the accident of birth
in a nearby state
I've made my way
to the place I call home
the house built by my father's hands

no family is left
but the house breathes
with their heartbeats
glows with their wood,
wrought ironwork
stone seawall and
paintings on the walls

we humans like to think
we make choices
based on ocean gleam
autumn blaze
winter quiet
or breathless
blossoming spring

but the truth is
we struggle
on our way upstream
like salmon
to the homeplace
where we will be content
to die.

Considering Exodus

Would you consider running away
far from northern snowshine,
turn your back on fishermen
steaming home at sundown?
Could you ignore the flash of wing
at the last empty feeder,
step around the flower bed
where crocuses and snowdrops sleep,
dig out dead ashes from the cold stove
that should glow red
and pop their shadows on the walls,
say goodbye to old spruce sentinels
standing guard on the rocky shore,
face away from books, ship models, rubber boots,
the Sou'wester hanging in the hall?

Go ahead. Close the door that sticks in rain,
hang the key on a nail in the shed
and run as fast as you can
run away, run away, run
to a steamy place far south from home
and never look back again.
Try, if you will.
Go ahead, if you can.

I'm Staying

Summer's end
sweeps in on a mournful breeze.
Lyon's Turtleheads nod goodbye.
Stubborn tomatoes cling to the vines,
still green when it's time for us to leave.
This fall there will be no ending.
I'm staying here
for the rest of my days.
I refuse to go.

Defiant

My walls are scattered with paintings
by artists living and dead.
Softened by sienna and burnt umbra,
people who sat for their portraits
departed this world lifetimes ago.
Long-gone hands held brushes that left
glowing surf exploding in oil —
rendered in viridian, cerulean
and Prussian blue —
roaring out from driftwood frames,
tossing up misty spray
replying to curling foam
outside this morning's window.
Shelves in the room are crowded with writings
by poets, most of them dead.
Their words still echo in the dusty air,
arise from ragged pages,
and quiver up on the ceiling.
Images and words of beauty
will vibrate through timeless tomorrows
unending, undying,
defiant.

My Father Lives Here

My father died years ago but still lives with me
in this house.
I imagine he breathes
tonight, every night,
and in the morning's first light
he hammers the woodstove tools
with brass knob wrought iron handles
smiling with rub of countless fingers.
He curls the metal lamp
into the shape of an anchor,
bends the bread baskets
and tin coffin trays,
nails the varnished wooden walls
with familiar old knots
and fastens the cupboards with hinges.
Evenings in the kitchen
he slides the ribbed sweater I knitted for him
over his head,
tucks his ancient fiddle
under his chin, tunes up
and plays my favorite song.
Everything he made speaks to me
in vibrating silent memory.
On winter nights, hot water gurgles
through the pipes along the baseboards
purring soft lullabies.
Forty-eight years after his death,
my father is here in the house with me now,
his arm around my shoulder
keeping me company
as dusk creeps on.

Reflection

The mirror must lie
that can't be my face
staring back at me in the bathroom
with amazement and shock

Laugh line parentheses
an extra fold under the chin
eyebrows invisible
How could this happen?

Is it my mother peering out
of the shadowy glass
a cruel trick of deception
to betray me at last?

My mother has been gone
for many years
I thought she had faded
away into darkness

I recall a blemish
at the nape of her neck
a birthmark, she called it
a dark purple mystery

Today I reach back
to a dry itchy patch of skin
at the same place of my own
and scratch it.

Internal Correspondence

Who am I, really?
Where do I live?
How do I get my mail?
Not just letters in the tin box
at the head of the driveway —
I mean the real messages
that reach deep inside my being
where I hide my mind.
What glows in the dark
when I shut my eyes?
When an entity somewhere
in the black universe
beams me a silent question
that must be important,
how do I send out my answer?
Is there anyone out there who hears?
Or am I just shouting alone
in the dark,
as always?

Where Does it Come From?

How does the seed of a poem begin?
What starts the thought to sprout from darkness,
poke up, spread leaves,
explode into blossom?

Do capsules exist before birth
in the mind?
What does the child hear
and carry for years in growing,
ideas dormant for decades
before at last rising to bloom?

Do poems leak out from shallow sleep
unspoken memories deeply bruised,
rivers of words overflowing the mind
rhythms echoing steady heartbeats
musical lines loosely restrained
begging for a finger's release?

A poem curls a thought in widening circles
clicks back on itself
like a pebble in the spoke of a wheel
that rotates round and round
repeats itself and bursts out at last
dizzy and raging to be freed.

Maybe the poem is a Touch-Me-Not Plant with stems
that curlycue tight into springs,
shoot out seeds when the bud is touched.
Is this how a poem flies out into air
for others to gather, hold, and plant,
or ignore, and turn into dust?

Alice in Technoland

I wander through the huge array
of puzzling items on display:

I-Pad, I-Phone, Kindle, Nook
all to wipe out pens and books

for kids or adults, toys or tools?
designed for techies or for fools

to gulp up empty minutes while
in waiting rooms or grocery aisles?

They beam out signals through the air
to other brains, I know not where.

They buzz and jitter in my hand,
lost here in a foreign land.

I am like Alice, all alone,
no GPS to lead me home.

Dropped Stitches

I have spent years knitting and purling
for loves now gone:

argyle socks for the teenaged boy
whose mother shrank them
to a fifth of their size
in a hot water wash

the maroon sweater with the starburst pattern
for the college man
who took another girl
to the Harvard-Yale game

the navy number for the sea-going man
lanolin-oiled to shed spray and rain —
I wonder whatever happened to it
when the captain returned to his wife —

the fiery red pullover for my first husband
ultimately cast off, alas

the Irish fisherman's knit
for the guy who moved in
with another woman
just as I finished the sleeves

the blue cable knit for my son
half finished before he died
and completed years later
to wear as my own

I sit by the Christmas tree tonight
purling and cabling
trying to work up an easy
one-piece vest before sunrise

for one who is probably
my final Ulysses

I'm thinking that maybe I should unravel
the yarn every night like Penelope
and be done
with knitting for men.

Message

Three black shadows glide
over the dampening updraft
wheeling
wheeling
wheeling.
Riding wet November wind,
crows settle into the witch's broom
at the crest of a naked spruce tree.
Sinister ebony watchmen
cloaked in shiny capes
break the shivering silence
with three harsh warnings,
alerting cousins deep in the woods.

Their signals are returned
as three sharp answers
clearly repeated,
echoes from distant treetops:

Message received and understood.

Land-Locked

Slouched in a wooden chair
at the edge of sea, midsummer,
knitting yarn idle in my lap,
day after day
I watch a sailboat catch the breeze
wishing I could guide her tiller
out there, far away from land.

This day a young and slippery seal
pops his head above the waves,
round eyes glowing wide,
sparkling with sympathy.
My own glance locks with his,
a long moment of meaning,
exchange of understanding.

On the ninth night at dusk
I will waltz down to the shore,
shed seven tears of an Orkney wife
and wait for the shining Selkie boy
to wade out of the evening water,
peel wet sealskin from his body
and lead me down to his home in the deep.

# Changing Landscapes

The Old Garden Remains

Tall fierce grass tries to smother
Daylilies bravely outliving
the gardening hands of a grandmother
the empty hole surviving
the old red house that sagged
windows carefully removed
ridgepoles roughly dragged
away with the patched and leaking roof
making space for a designer's mansion.
All that is left is the long sweep
of waving field, Northeast wind,
and the Atlantic Ocean,
where Irises nod and Forget-me-nots weep.

The House Comes Down

Newcomers from another state
are tearing down the tired house.
Old timbers groan with each hard thud
of the giant wrecking beast.
A cornerstone moans and shudders
with steaming wheezes of the shovel.
The roof flinches, squawks, and falls.
The graceful fieldstone chimney
is the last to stand,
still proud, defiant, at quitting time.
Now, far across the ragged field,
woods darken in fading daylight.
Look quickly! Among the trees
two translucent shadows flicker.
On closer look, they could almost be—
almost—but not quite—two old people
hidden, watching, sighing,
grieving.

Flood Waters

The river
begins
innocently
as a trickle
then every hour
it laps farther up
the river banks, swells
like a breast filling with milk
groans and heaves itself up on its shoulder
the same way volcanic magma curls
hissing and bubbling over its crest
gulps up the incessant rain
rolls into a shouting roar, a battering ram
like the front ranks of an advancing army.
Workers rush to loosen the cranks
that open the straining levees' gates.
Thundering mountains of muddy water
burst over the helpless fields, fan out
like a drowned woman's hair —
the luckless farmers sacrifice
to save the cities and homes
swallowed and dragged
downstream.

Two Trees

Five cat spruces, a hundred years old,
still shade the house from noonday sun,
protect us from winds and winter cold,
filter red sky when days are done.

The oldest trunks are coated with moss,
branches bare, needles brown.
More broken limbs the gales have tossed
are severed arms upon the ground.

A planted youngster from woods nearby
in years of sun, grew thirty feet.
Its upturned arms reached high to the sky
and an old tree stretched a hand to greet.

A sparrow hopped from old branch to new —
from two fingers, a spark of life on cue.

The Brook

For years, my own ancient stream
rippled its way among the thickets
from scratchy arms of uncut trees
to mossy fields of wild blueberries
out of shadows into sunshine
under brilliant August heat
winding down from hill to sea
a bubbling guide for my feet.

If ever I would wander, lost
in tangled stand of evergreens,
fluttering water would guide me on
through the pathless underbrush
of sunless virgin woods,
my ear trained toward the hum
of lobster boats not far away
at its ending, on the bay.

Now it slips through treeless house lots,
banks of fancy landscaped lawns,
creative glittering designs
hand-carved shapes with leaning ferns
a cuckold's prideful winning plan
chuckling nouveau manmade art,
a selling point to raise the rate
of expensive modern real estate.

Nothing on Earth is Meant to Stay

Our dirt road was once a quiet trail
that wound to homes along the shore
but it could not stay for long;
the neighbors gave it to the town
to pave with tar, repair and plow.
Now it teems with feet and many wheels,
workers' trucks, black exhaust,
spectators of the ocean views.
Wild plants and birdsong left the woods,
chain saws took the whispering pines,
the hidden tree house disappeared.
Along with youth, it could not stay.
This road has cast off innocence.
Miles away, in faded fields
farmhouses and decaying barns
give way to rotting timber,
collapse in lonely piles of firewood.
Cellar holes are last to go,
for stones are ponderously slow.
Old folks' names are lost in clouds
as sea wipes footprint from the sand.
Ocean tides, the moon and stars
the only ones in time remain.
No earthbound life is meant to stay.

Far, Far Away

Sleeping Under Mosquito Netting

At dawn in Yogyakarta
daylight fingers its way through
the giant leafy hands
that fold
themselves around my balcony
screening it
from the rising heat.
It holds birds I cannot name
that twitter sleepily
in the damp lush green.

A muezzin's high voice peals out
clear and plaintive
from a rickety wooden minaret
across the road.
Its mournful pitch rises and falls
in heavy air.
Every note glides up
and slides down a scale
wavering, quivering
in octaves unfamiliar to my western ear
calling the faithful to prayer.

I roll over, heavy with sleep
encased in gauzy clouds
of mosquito netting
draped over my four-posted bed.
The large ceiling fan
rotates lazily
stirring the air.
Fluttering white billows of net
surround me
to keep out winged demons
and other infidels.

Lago Maggiore

Sharp-toothed mountains hover over the Italian border
in a protective embrace of Lake Maggiore.
The sweet scent of dead rose petals
floats on bottomless glacial water.

Grand hotels line up along the shores
like full-blown matrons
standing proudly in receiving lines,
petunias bursting from their bosomy balconies.

In the placid water, centuries old, we
can almost see rippling reflections
of ghostly women with parasols
strolling down the lakeside promenades.

Borromeo Castle looms on the island offshore:
gilt-framed paintings reflected in slippery marble floors,
hanging gardens, statuary, wine cellars,
white peacocks fanning feathers on the lawn.

We can almost hear the echoes
of court violinists playing for masked ladies
and gentlemen collared with lace
under flickering chandeliers.

All this glitter shone when
what is now the Coast of Maine
awoke as a wild rough wooded outpost for
loggers, hunters, trappers, and traders.

One new land giving birth in the world,
an old one, fading and dying.

The Biggest and Most Silent

Everything is BIG in Moscow:
statues, hotels, apartment houses, palaces,
offices, the KGB and the Kremlin.
Three levels of escalators carry us
to the deepest bowels of the city,
the Metro, loaded with frescoes,
gold leaf statues, mosaics.
G.U.M.*, the State Department Store,
multi levels and alleyways,
mostly empty because of prices
three times higher than those in the towns.
Traffic gridlocks rival China and India
for the title of worst in the world.

Ultimately we come upon the Tsar Bell:
supposed to weigh two hundred tons,
largest in the world
like everything else in the capital of Russia,
cast from other melted-down iron
to announce Easter, and deaths of Tzars.
Too heavy to mount in the bell tower,
it sat still in the square when a fire advanced,
turning the steel red hot.
Cold water was poured upon it in panic,
it cracked and a huge piece burst off,
leaving it a monument to useless sound.

Other bells, not quite so large,
were melted down and recast as a cannon,
the largest caliber in the world,
that never fired a single shot.

So now we view
the largest bell in the world
that never has rung
and the biggest gun
that never was fired.
We are left here with
the terrible weight of silence.

*G.U.M. pronounced "Goom"

Iceberg
St. Anthony's Harbor, Newfoundland

Where do you come from?
How far?
How cold?
I'm told
that your ice
five thousand years old
shuddered, groaned,

broke away in despair
from a forsaken land
three years ago,
drifted with winds
on a slow ocean current
to the narrow mouth
of this quiet harbor.

Countless air bubbles
encased in your clear face
float shining
above the water.

What ancient creature
breathed the air
in those age-old bubbles
and possibly sank
forever
to the bottom of the sea?

Below the surface
lurks a formidable titan
seven times as deep
as the ice peaks
slicing the sky overhead.

How terrifying is the monster
that lies beneath
with deadly teeth.

The Shattered Balkans
One Region Split into Seven*

We drive away
from sunburnt bodies
on beaches and ride inland
leave sails on blinding waters
sweep up to tiny stone farms
on the hillsides
small families rake
rows of cabbages and tend
olive trees, trying to
lift themselves up
from oppressors,
dictators, murderers
to call themselves
by the names
of their seven countries
to step over the rubble
of destruction and
bodies in unmarked fields
where last year
fathers and uncles
shot each other
over senseless allegiance
to misunderstandings
never forgotten
generations of vicious vendettas
in order to stand up and say
"This is my beloved country."

*Disputedly: Albania, Bosnia, Croatia, Hercegovina, Montenegro, Sarajevo, Slovenia

The Boys of Orkney

An Orkney boy is not born for the land.
His destiny is outward bound to the sea.

His ancestors left for Hudson Bay,
some searched for a passage slicing through land,
sailed out with whalers to the South Seas.
His grandfathers signed on at Scapa Flow
or disappeared into the Merchant Marine.
Most are gone from the isle forever.

Where are the Orkney boys today?
Now steering trawlers into the wind
for herring and prawns in the oncoming dark.
Mist caresses the ghost town of stone,
whispers through twisting streets of Stromness,
empty now on a sleeping Sabbath.

Wind swept away all the trees of Orkney;
the sea has taken the restless boys.

An Old Woman's Farewell to St. Kilda
The End of an Island Community

Our old home lies so far out of sight
past the western curve of the earth
locked from the mainland by Atlantic surf
alone, with only ghosts for its people.

For hundreds of years it breathed with neighbors
held intact by an island parliament
of fishermen, crofters, hunters who scaled
cloud-covered cliffs for gannets, puffins, and fulmar.

Held together by prayers and sermons,
women spun, wove, cared for children and elders.
Able men and women shared the burdens,
strong enough to support us all.

But illness cloaked over old and young,
survival hung on trembling threads,
too far from the mainland for help in the winter.
Young people hungered for life far away.

With only the aging preacher and wife
to teach us and pray to keep us alive,
held hostage by a tight-fist religion,
we feared what lay outside our shores.

We finally knew we were bound for extinction
and I was the last to sign the petition,
asking the laird to move us ashore,
and the steamers approached on that bitter day.

Our few belongings were bundled in blankets.
Men loaded sheep, two scared highland cattle.
They wheeled me down to the shore in a cart.
I slipped out and limped a few steps at the end.

It seemed like we were running from home.
The clouds hung over the cliffs, forlorn.
I would not be able to die on my island,
the beloved place where I was born.

Duval Street, Key West

The street at night is a roaring river
tumbling up and down its banks
in thunders of laughter,
shouts, greetings, invitations,
a torrent of sound:
marimbas, guitars, keyboard, sax,
voices crooning through the darkening air—
music-makers, dancers, jugglers, jesters.

Walkers pause to read signs on stores:
Don't say cheap, say inexpensive
Fast Buck Freddie's
Shirley Can't Surf
Lost Weekend Liquor Store
The Most Comfortable Toe Rings You'll Ever Wear.

A drag queen in short-shorts
invites people into the Aqua Dance
"Next show in ten minutes, folks!"
Another in a white robe and halo
wades through clouds of supersuds,
asks us to try drinks poured over freezer snow.
A youth with a flute sits on the sidewalk,
"Take a picture of my dog and leave him a tip."
A figure lurks in a black cape, muttering
"Come upstairs to Grumpy Dick's."
A little old man from the Full Deliverance Gospel Church
plays hymns on a worn out violin.

Hog's Breath Saloon,
The Red Garter, Green Parrot
make the street a cacophony
of dancers, actors, pitch men,
bar flies and die-hards.
Deep into the night
planets whirl across the glowing sky
and disappear into dawn.

The morning after the night before,
the river slows down to a trickle.
The sun glimmers through shimmering air,
noise fades to a chick's peep and a rooster's crow.
Shop doors are shuttered and
couples push strollers with rosy babies
up the sleepy silent sidewalk
on the street they call Duval.

Boundaries

We don't always understand boundaries:
the borders, the edges, the lines.
Who draws them?
There are miles of high thick walls
or fences of invisible barbed wire.

Men have created dangerous borders
stepped over by slaves to Canada,
workers from Sonora, Mexico,
and checkpoints all over the world.
Crossing the lines, a conscious decision,
might mean either freedom or death.

There are mile limits
even in the seamless ocean,
to keep fishermen in or out.
It is important to know
where we are supposed to stop.
Is there a beginning on the other side?

The Sami people never understood borders.
Disregarding the Cold War, they drove their herds
across the tundra from Finland to Russia
and back again with no questions.
Guards never asked them for papers.

Wolves do not understand boundaries either.
Reintroduced by men to live and thrive
in Yellowstone Park, they cross
over the borders, not knowing the rules,
and are shot.

Inisheer Sweater

Look offshore to the Aran Islands
Hulking up from Galway Bay
Whispering messages through the mist
Echoes whistling down the hillsides
Beckoning us to come away.

Kittiwakes squeal and reel in circles
In and out of their nests in cliffs
Rooks croak their hard sarcastic laughs
Like crones predicting violent death
Warning of predestined loss.

On Inisheer all the women
Knit their creamy woolen sweaters
In patterns as distinct as names
Stitches to redeem their sins
And reclaim the bodies of their men.

Praying with the clicking needles
No one will climb the stony strand
Bearing a body from the shore
Wrapped in a dripping sea-soaked sweater
Knitted in the family design.

I brood about the fisherman's sweater
I knitted for my only son
Who died before I finished it
Bad luck, predestined, fate unfair
Or I forgot to knit a prayer.

The Swimming Sleeper

I sidestroke down the Atlantic Ocean
from north to south in my sleep
flutterkick through the crowds of Europe
rise above the clouds and roll
onto my back, float over Siberia
breast stroke to graves of Argentina
skim over crests of the heaving Pacific
crawl along ragged coasts of Africa
and keep on swimming
around the world.

Good People, Old and Young

Light in the Window

At the head of the harbor
on the top of the hill
stands an old frame house,

white paint peeled off
after years of winters
facing out toward a stormy sea.

Every day at dusk
a light streams out a signal
from the second floor window.

For years, the man trudged down to the wharf,
boarded the biggest ship in the harbor,
steamed out to fish on the Gulf of Maine.

After fifty years of his absence,
his wife still limps up the stairs every night
to flick on the light in the second-floor window,

expecting the ship to round the point,
a voice to crackle over the radio,
and footsteps to crunch up the hill
in the snow.

Two Young Mothers with Babies

The elevated train thunders out of the T station,
clatters over the Charles Street Bridge.
Traffic idles for endless minutes,
cars coughing out choking fumes.
Wind hurls dust from the blistering roadway.
A young woman strides down from Beacon Hill,
holds her large brimmed straw hat
close to her sunglasses with one hand,
her long runway figure
draped in a black ankle-length dress.
She leans into the wind, pushing a slick baby pram
around the cars with her other arm.
She plows headlong to the park on the river,
eyes on the whipping clouds and white sails
that flit over the water.
She plots a course toward Storrow Drive,
open air for her child
on the cool edge of the city.

On the same sunny day
two hundred miles north, in coastal Maine,
a young woman in blue jeans
fresh from Morning Dew Farm,
smiling pink cheeks, fair hair tied back,
weighs out shell peas at the Farmers' Market.
Her infant, suspended in a cotton sling,
suckles at the swollen morning breast
under her mother's sun-bleached shirt.
An awning protects them with gentle shade.
A towel drapes modestly over the child's head
as the woman hands the bag of fresh peas
over the wooden table.

Here we see two young mothers,
far apart in so many ways,
on the same summer morning,
both breathing in the coastal breeze
each, instinctive in maternal mission,
tenderly doing the best she can.

Deadly Conflict
The Battle of the Boxer and the Enterprise
September 5, 1813

We are two hundred years too late
to witness the conflict out on the bay:
the fight of the Boxer and the Enterprise,
the smoke that billowed into the sky.
We stand here now on the point of land
once named by the natives Pemaquid.
Safe on shore the onlookers stood
hearing explosions, breathing the smoke,
not sure what the bloodshed was all about.
Those who watched, knew nothing of reasons,
were drawn to the shore by the smell of danger.
They did not know that, at age twenty-seven,
this was the captain's first commission.
Blyth nailed his colors to Boxer's mast,
Burrows maneuvered his ship alongside,
and two young captains too young to die
ordered the carronades to fire.
Boxer suffered the first of the broadsides.
Her topgallants shredded, exploded in flames,
her main topmast was split into pieces,
tons of sail and spars thundered down.
Crippled, the Boxer could not change her course.
A cannonball sliced Captain Blyth in two.
A musket shot pierced Captain Burrows' hip.
He sat dying on the Enterprise deck,
refused to accept Britain's sword of honor,
ordered it to Blyth's home be sent.
Burrows' final words, "I die content."
On Munjoy Hill, the captains lie,
two brave young men too young to die.

Jane Austin's Girls

Miss Austin knew the formula.
Eager girls under twenty
and anxious ones a few years older,
breasts pushed high in latest fashion,
tight ringlets under bulging bonnets
amble down bucolic lanes
swinging parasols and
tiptoeing nimbly over stiles.
Their eyes scan the stately mansions
scouting unattached young gentlemen
of inherited wealth from mysterious sources
back from military service where
they strut in tailored officer uniforms,
likely never having seen a battle.

The hunted quarry must be handsome
and skilled in social dancing,
of higher station than her family's.
(A country pastor or school master
does not get past the starting gate.)
The girl must be mannerly, reserved,
pretty, and not very smart.
It helps if she plays the piano,
though not exceptionally well.

Daughters gossip and giggle giddily
in stuffy drawing rooms with teacups
or flirt on rural walks and picnics.
If they are lucky, older relatives
or parents' friends of means
whisk them "out" in coach-and-fours

to glittering towns in social seasons.
Parents push to orchestrate matches
in augmentation of family fortunes,
but love always wins the race.

The man-hunts conclude
with proposals of marriage accepted.
This is where all the novels end.
What happens ever after
is anyone's guess.
Miss Austin didn't play the game herself.
She wrote her way to fame,
and doomed herself to spinsterhood.

Eventful Day in an Edwardian Family

Rosebud in a small crystal vase,
tea, and paper with news of the day.
Lady Mae has breakfast in bed
delivered on a silver tray.

Her lady's maid appears on cue,
helps arrange the daughter's tresses.
Oh, what decisions must be made
now to choose from morning dresses.

The Lord confers with family broker,
inspects the crofters on his farms,
looks forward to a shooting party,
admires new roadster in the barn.

Son gallops out with boots and crop,
how else do gentry spend their time?
Reading, visiting, sipping tea,
awaiting dinner bells to chime.

Maids hook buttons, clasp on jewels.
Footmen brush off flakes from backs.
All descend to formal dinner.
Is there anything this family lacks?

Outbound Alone

A mysterious energy surged within,
pushed Schweitzer into the African jungle.
A similar drive sent Mother Theresa
into the rotting stench of Calcutta.

An unstoppable force winged Beverly Sills
from Brooklyn up to the dazzling Met.
Sir Hillary climbed above the clouds
propelled by an inner relentless strength.

Slocum, alone in an elderly boat,
set out to sail around the world.
Frank Lloyd Wright was drawn to create
a house hanging over a waterfall.

Yet one man gave up Wall Street to sleep
and end his days on an island with sheep.

Unfinished Gardener

She was struck down in July
when the begonias bloomed.

Sweet peas and lavender flourished
as she sighed and sank into her bed.

Impatiens and weeds overflowed the border
as summer grew, waned, and paraded out.

Lilies wondered where their caretaker was
but plodded on bravely without her.

The Gardener was swept into earth, sky,
clouds, wind, and water

when her Yule Cactus opened
at the end of November.

Summer in Miami

The woman and her man report
they've been living in Miami year-round
for sixty years
probably in one of those
high rises
that block off
all views of the sea.

Questioned about the August weather,
she explains that summer is called
the "indoor time"
of their lives.

This might man they don't ever go out
except to hop from air-conditioned rooms
to air-conditioned taxis, pharmacies,
to air-cooled restaurants,
hospitals, mortuaries, funeral homes
or receptions with circling fans
swinging on the ceilings.

Maybe this means they never breathe
untreated air
hear bird calls or ripples of waves
feel sand between their toes
smell bougainvillea
or glance up to the sky
until winter
when finally

it's the "outdoor time"
of their lives.

Banjo
Villanelle

I always wanted to give him a banjo
I thought it would finally bring out some cheer
to my sad father, long years ago

He played for the folks with his fiddle and bow
nostalgic tunes they all asked to hear
I always wanted to give him a banjo

There was hardly a tune that he didn't know
The notes from his fiddle rang out pure and clear
played by my father those long years ago

His sadness swelled and overflowed
I thought I could make his cares disappear
I always wanted to give him a banjo

People sang all the words they would know
or hum sad ballads and wipe away tears
inspired by his fiddle long years ago

When I finally had enough money to go
to the music store, he'd been dead for a year.
I always wanted to give him a banjo
my poor, sad father, long years ago

Good Old Men

I have known some good old men
the finest men in anyone's world—
no longer wild or temperamental
no pouting or pursuing cloud formations,
skirts, or changing tides.
Poets, philosophers, scientists, friends
patient and positive
no longer robust but stout of mind
remembering sweetness of yesterday:
Silent John with his pipe in his teeth
suffered students with straying thoughts;
Tom, gentle companion in shadow
at Robert Frost's northern farm;
Francis, blind, a head bursting with poems,
eager to hear the words from pages,
humble, grateful, kind;
Alden, recalling minutia of youth,
mountains, deserts, canyons and oceans
overflowing with achievements.
They all listen and endure,
do not lecture, judge, complain
of blindness, loss, disappointment, pain.
Hold on to today, let go of sorrow
and never, ever, mention tomorrow.

School Reunion

Here we are,
the last of us still standing.
Can't help viewing the old photos.
Look at the opening lineup:
football players at the Thanksgiving Game.
The fullback in the front row, fifth from left
squinting into the sun
died five years ago.
The coach and the quarterback two rows behind him
were gone the following spring.
How about the girl who twisted
under her partner's arm
in the swing dance step at the party
and her breast popped out of the strapless dress?
How humiliating for her
and embarrassing for her friends.
She'll never remember it now
in Alzheimer's shadowland.
Where is the shining beauty queen
or the shy girl who became a librarian?
What became of the sad boy who ran the projector
or the funny guy who played the spoons?
The very bright girl, front row,
her hand constantly waving
to answer the questions
has disappeared with the rest of them.
So many are gone
except from memories.
Those of us left
turn the pages, sadly,
and mark them absent.

Photograph of Innocence

Yarmouth Harbor on the Cape
fall of 1970
late this afternoon
Brad and Blacky-Brown
have paused on the boardwalk
that stretches over muddy flats.
Brad is thirteen, smiling
unsuspecting
his arms around the dog.
I am sad to tell him that
his dad is soon to die.

Hide and Seek

At a shouted signal
the children scattered
disappeared to hiding places
in the closet of winter coats
also deep in the hamper
among wet towels
or behind the drapes
and under the beds

The boy who wished
to be a girl
snuggled the flaxen
headed doll
his favorite
under his sleeve
and scurried out
to the unused barn

stirring up
a mini tornado
of dust motes
that swirled
in the dying
summer sunlight
Later we found him
smothered

under a stack
of heavy quilts
We figured out
he had won the game
The child
who had hidden the longest
from himself and us
was dead.

Boys at the Back of the Bus

The old yellow school bus wheezes and stops
Octangular signs flip out from its flanks
Arthritic wings warn drivers behind
Unschooled in the secrets of privilege and rank

A young boy outweighed by his oversized pack
Slides safe to the shadowy middle seat
Unspoken admission as small and unworthy
Demeanor submissive, quiet, discreet

A covey of girls swoops up the steps
They fill in the seats with feminine fluttering
Hopping to spaces saved for others
Ignoring the driver's impatient muttering

At the end of the route the big boys arrive
Middle school heroes of athletic fame
No backpacks or books, toting only their pride
With practiced expressions of high disdain

On purpose they make the bus driver wait
Stroll to the end of their royalty track
Past unclaimed spaces and admiring faces
To the honored last seats of the bus in the back.

Fishing in the Rain

Three days of rain
on the island
and the boys are restless.
First a young one
strides down to the dock
with his box and tackle.
Then two bigger boys
arrive with their poles
silently
to join him.
What do they care
if the sky leaks drizzle?
Locked in the house
is not a possible choice
when they could be plumbing
the watery mysteries
that swirl deep, dark
beneath the pilings.

First Encounter
A METCO* Child Meets the Ocean

The boy awakes winter days in the city,
shivers in dark at the lonely bus stop.
His mother insists it's worth the try
to reach out for an education.
He rides, half asleep, for over an hour
to my fifth grade class in a suburban school.

Months drag on toward lightening skies
till one sun-filled day in June
an old yellow bus groans up the highway
hauling our class to study tide pools
an hour away in the wind of North Shore.
Children flood from the wheezing bus,
spill, ecstatic, up the thorny path
to the monstrous boulders of Halibut Point.

"I can SMELL the sea!" the boy exclaims,
impatient, approaching the shore,
overgrown by wild berries.
"I can HEAR the sea!" he shouts
to no one and everyone,
scrambling up the hill
through waving beach roses.

Ragged weeds give way at last
to the shiny overturned bowl of sky.
A scream erupts, unbidden
from somewhere deep in himself.
"I CAN SEE THE OCEAN!!!"
He throws himself on a mountainous rock
that rises wet with the tide.
He is stunned by the noisy power of surf,
a glittering moment he will never forget
and decades later, neither will I.

*A program begin in 1966 for bussing inner city children to school in outlying suburbs.

Winter Recess Lament

I have Andrew's snowpants on
and he has put on mine,
so off will come our velcro boots
and we get out of line.

My right boot's on the wrong foot,
the left looks like a flipper.
I have to take my mittens off
so I can zip my zipper.

I need to stop to blow my nose.
The mittens go back, one by one.
When I'm finally in my outdoor clothes,
recess is all done.

Darkness and Nightmares

Dreams

Visions whirl at night
Tricksters streak across the mind
Dancers in the dark

Phantom Boatman

There's a rattling grate of a hull
on the stony beach nearby
above the reeking seaweed.
Someone is dragging a skiff

down to the low water line
where it will bob on the surface
waiting for the oarsman
to toss in the pail and fishing pole.

I rise from my chair,
walk to the edge of the seawall.
In my fantasy it is my son
out on a quest for mackerel.

But of course it can't be —
he's been gone from this world
for nineteen years.
He'll never again head out on the bay.

You'd think, after all this time
I'd ignore the grating of hull on gravel
when someone drags it
down into the tide.

Writer's Nightmare

Under a cloud-like dream
I work in haste at an old-fashioned machine.
Ten more pages are typed
complete with four carbon copies.
I twist the knob to roll them out and
am shocked that the top sheets are blank.
The ink has all dried up
but carbon copies remain intact.
I flick through to catch page numbers.
Thousands of small black flakes
tumble out, scatter in all directions.
Little black words flutter all over the desktop,
the floor, the blood-spattered carpet—
tiny black butterflies, all of them dead
except for one. It stretches out its wings
on my exhaled breath
and flies away from daylight
in a gallant, desperate escape.

Ascending a Maze to Escape

I am lost before dawn
in a house on the eastern shore
with countless inner wooden stairs
that twist and fold around corners.
I climb up, but cannot find my way down.
Closed in by walls of fragrant pine,
ceilings of different heights,
endless doors that open and close
on empty rooms and still more doors.
I can't seem to retrace my steps.
One room has bunks like those in a schooner,
such as coffins too tight for sitting up.
Some slide in and out like bureau drawers,
or files in a morgue for bodies.
I hear laughing, chattering voices
behind closed doors, yet
every time I open one after another,
no one is there.
A man I know lives in this house,
somewhere,
but he is gone most of the time
and I cannot find him.
Nowhere are there openings for
sunlight or air,
except on the uppermost floor.
A wide, unfinished window
without any glass
allows me to gaze out at last
on a loud and tempting sea
foaming far below me.

Letting Go

I am glad
my mind is clear so I
can write my thoughts on paper
I can breathe the northwest wind
that carries the earthy smell
of spring thaw

I wish that
I could walk throughout the world
for two more decades
reaching out to others,
enfolding friends and enemies
into my arms

but there are
old dilemmas, decisions
mistakes I must lug
like a backpack of scrap iron
or rocks in my pockets
to the edge of a river

it would be good
to write thanks, gladness, regrets and wishes
on tissue scraps: pink, aqua, indigo, gold
release them from a cliff
to spin off as airborne sails
into the accepting sky

Denouement

Emerging from artists and craftsmen
earning our keep in haphazard classrooms,
I thought I'd write an enormous novel
but eventually lived it instead,
not sugar coated
but crusted in salt.
My book had unbound scribbled pieces
stapled together
in looseleaf patterns:
a young girl running up blind alleys,
retreating,
losing her way,
clinging to cliffs by raw fingernails,
digging her hands
into fertile dirt,
drifting over all the world's waters.
This novel had everything:
doubt and decisions,
passion, adventure, tears, a few laughs,
a relieved sign
on the final page
at the edge of a northern sea.

Dark Island

The schooner's sails were furled up tight,
she was anchored on the sheltered shore,
floating calm in fading light
off an island I had never seen before.

The whaleboat took some of us ashore
and landed us on rattling stones
so if we wished, we could explore
the winding paths in woods alone.

Those fit and swift soon swept ahead
leaving me to run behind,
not sure which winding paths to tread
without a light or clue to find.

In my island dream I lost the trail
and was abandoned out at sea.
At dawn the schooner hoisted sail
and drifted off without me.

Reruns

I wake too early to get out of bed
Midnight thoughts spin through my head
All the ignorant mistakes
Wrong decisions, muddled takes
Scenes I wish I could rerun
Replay them now as happy ones
Bad choices that I can't forget
Lost in a forest of regret
I was another person then
That self died and regrew when
I emerged, shed aging skin
Revealing a new life within.

Maine Winter and Other Seasons

Making the Turn

There comes a time
with dependable rhythm
every year
late in August
when the wind turns around,
blows in air from the north
to chill the bay
and the year turns its face
away from summer.

Monarch butterflies
ripple down to zinnias that bend
toward late afternoon sun,
bank their wings
and lean into the last leg
of their unavoidable flight plan.

Some time in every life
there comes that inevitable turn
when we face away . . .
I can't be sure
when that moment was for me.

October Wind

Red, russet, gold leaves
Flutter from the blowing trees
Sparkling jewels spin

Daylight Savings Time

Sunset is early
Daylight flies away too soon
The dark is rising

New Season

Three days before Solstice
I stride along the winter road
past vacation cottages
empty at the turn of the year.

The sun sinks over the opposite shore
into darkness, bleeds colors
that creep over the blood-red bay
and redden the saddening snow.

I pull up my scarf
pick up the pace
defy the freezing air
with my breath

turn into the path
to the only home
glowing with lights
open the door

enter at last the welcoming hope
of the woodstove
the throbbing pulse
of a new season.

Winter Solstice

Darkness hits us over the head
like a clap of thunder
leaves us gasping for light
as if under water
paddling in panic
a swim for the surface

Winter tromps in
plunks its fat backside
flat on our chest
so we can't catch our breath
buried alive
six feet under the ice

Rise of Coastal Water

The full moon at dawn
is a giant ball of ice
suspended for an ominous moment
at the fringe of the western shore.
A message from the Arctic
creeps across the freezing sea.
The outermost islands,
ringed by vapor,
float, disconnected
from water or land
ready to dissolve
into the winter sky.
The highest water of the year
floods over the seawall.
Salty fingers reach out
and warn us to retreat.
At winter's dawn we come to know
once more the dark is rising.

Mornings Below Zero

Cold air shrinks us back under goosedown,
ice seals us up on January mornings,
locks us out of all necessary chores.
Deep, deep cold slows down our blood
like half-frozen, pulsing, slushy tidepools.
It persuades us to wait a few more hours,
close our eyes, take shallow breaths,
spend long mornings in bottomless sleep
before stirring, rising, lighting the stove
to perk two cups of bubbling coffee,
cover our bodies with layers of wool,
and force ourselves into the winter world
out of hibernation.

Winter Warfare

Snow crept eastward to the coast,
a seething silent panther
from the Great Lakes, snarling,
while a wildcat storm clawed its way
up the shoreline from the south.
They leapt at each other, screaming
with deadly claws unsheathed.
Two weather systems, untamed beasts,
enemies for centuries,
faced off and clashed,
whipped wind around
to explosive whirlpools
ice and snow
like fur flying.
War uninvented by mankind
without the help of human strength,
we mortals could only run and hide.
They tore the sky and earth to shreds
in violent rage
and chased each other to exhaustion
out to death at sea.

Winter Ghazal

Almost no one lives here in winter now.
Ghosts glide as smoke from a few old chimneys.

Rivers of air flow in giant wide circles,
Massive cold fronts inch down from the North.

Polar winds push souls to abandon their homes,
the living dead creep to steamy swamps in the South.

Some think old women choose to drift out to sea,
useless elders on floating islands of ice.

But Northern widows knit memories and dreams,
bank the fires in their hot iron stoves,

watch snow wrap around their single aloneness,
fearless women, not really lonely at all.

Winter Work

the light glows like diamonds
at the bottom of the year

the sun sets at the farthest point
on the western shore

whitecaps whip the steely bay
spindrift scatters off the crests

winter birds at early dark
hide in sheltering trees

we creatures curl up on our dens
enfolded warm into safekeeping

doors and windows seal up tight
we light the fires within

some of us hide and work with words
discovering all our songs inside

Mud Season Advice

When Dante wrote of Purgatory
it must have been in March:
a good time to get over whatever you've caught,
for in mud time nothing can get much worse.

Too late for skiing a snow-covered path, too early
to open windows or shake out quilts, too soon
to rig sailboats or start the peas.
The year-round wheel sinks deep into mud.

As winter stands up and gets ready to leave
like a tedious overstayed houseguest,
she hangs back at the door with many goodbyes.
You should join the wind in a sigh of relief.

Shake off your winter caul to breathe,
kick off your boots and step out barefoot.
Let the mud ooze up between your toes
and have an overdue talk with crocuses.

Spring Burst

The river is swollen
pregnant with trout
the race plummets
over rattling stones

buds on the pear tree
burst overnight
tender as nipples
on a thirteen-year-old girl

green creeps up
over the field
hesitant, unsure
tiptoeing over winter's death

earth holds its breath
waiting for
what is, to me,
the first day of the world.

The Sounds of Silence

> *Chief Seattle said*
> *in the white men's cities*
> *there was no place to hear*
> *the unfurling of leaves in spring*
> *or the rustle of insects' wings*
> —Chief Seattle's Lament 1864

Have you ever stopped to hear
the quiet sound of tulips opening,
the flutter of a small bird's feathers,
or the fuwoom! of the eagle

rising from the spruce branch,
the droplets popping down from the fog,
settling on pine needles, or
the purr of the outgoing tide?

Have you ever listened to the green sound
of the grass in the field
stretching up toward the sky,
the rhythmic snap of sunlight dancing off the bay

or the hum of the hot air at midsummer?
Try to listen—you might hear the stars
singing in their orbits
through the dark sky in winter.

Aging and Ending

Depending on the Tide

The tide, running out,
sucks life from the day.
The sea lies still
silent and thoughtful
holds its breath so long
it appears to be dead.

But it revives, turns
as if undecided,
circles in eddies,
slowly rises once again.

Incoming tide swells,
smiles at the shore,
creeps to embrace
those of us on land
who wait gratefully
for its kiss.

Barter

Spring was given away this year
not canceled or overlooked,
not deferred to a later date.
What happened to the greening season?
It evaporated
disappeared
over the distant shore.
But it could not be ignored.
I wanted to keep it, but I knew
that I could afford to let it go.
I bargained with each morning sun
and watched it creep away.
I was trading it for my life.

Summer dragged her fragrant skirt
through spiderwebs in the dew.
Gardens exploded with golden lilies
begging to be admired.
The beckoning tide whispered,
invited me into its depth,
but I refused.
I bartered my life's gleaming season
and in exchange
I turned my back on Darkness.

Radiation

The monster rattles and hums.
With invisible razor teeth
a metal dragon shoots fire from its jaws
to slay the killer cells, but also
loses good ones by mistake.
Twenty-eight battles down,
seven more to go.
After all is nearly ended,
my blood is still bubbling,
my bones are still smoldering,
the skin on my nose continues to blister.
This is war.

Waiting for an Answer

Tide eleven feet low, ready to turn.
I have followed it with my eyes
how many times in the last few days?
Dancing notes of Beethoven's Seventh
cheer me softly from the radio.
Seabirds skim over the still water,
some paddle in widening eddies,
dive beneath the surface, disappear
like memories quickly forgotten.
Miniature sparrows flit up and down
spruce branches on the shore,
busy, pecking for insects or seeds.
Hours move like molasses
as I wait for the telephone to ring
with the surgeon's message for me.

Youth Scramble

when I was young
I headed down unexplored paths
to dead ends
there were men who
wanted me to love them
to hold them
to stay
but I sent them
away
for reasons unknown
years later I wished
I could have them again
there were others
I reached for
but they turned their backs
I couldn't understand
what I was meant to do
I wanted to learn
everything spoken
or written
I wanted to help the world
in some way
or at least
make a dent in reality
I was a master
of wrong choices
and colossal mistakes
stumbling
like a blind animal
in a maze with no exit
fumbling

(continued)

for doorknobs to turn
trying on
futures for size
discarding them
for poor fit
changing reaching
sometimes letting go
infidelity amounted to
loving the wrong men
accomplishment finally meant
just muddling on

Another New Day

I awake slowly in dim gray light
before a January dawn.
My cat is urging me to arise,
poking her claws into my chest.
Soon she will join her partner
by the back window
eyeing sparrows in the trees.
I stretch my stiff legs, roll over,
gaze through the glass door
toward white caps on the water
and the snow-lined shore
across the bay.
I'm amazed and joyful
to be alive
another new day.

Too Old

There comes a limit to years
a greyhound can chase the rabbit
when she stops making money
for owners and gamblers
her life is certainly over unless
a kindhearted person saves her
and takes her home.

Farm horses can work the fields
only until they grow aged and lame
Old Ned got lucky
was turned out to pasture
most old fellows end up in a factory
turned into dog food
or glue.

The premier dancer in a national corps
must know when his knees and hips give out
he strains to lift the last ballerina
it's time to morph into
choreographer, director, executive
or ballet master
for eight-year-old kids.

I, too, am feeling the effects of age
no longer sustain the strength of the crawl
for a single lap of the swimming pool
am afraid to take the boat out alone
in case of a misstep I couldn't rely
on my arms to drag myself
over the gunwale.

It's That Time

You know you're getting old when
the charities that used to get your donations
once a year
start asking you to leave them legacies
until all the money runs out.

You know you're getting old when
catalogs come with ads for rollators
and bibs in case you dribble your food
and not just while dipping lobster
in melted butter.

Your nightly news is interrupted
for medical breakthroughs with fatal side effects,
and you start getting newsletters
on how to restore your sex life,
especially without a partner.

Your mail warns of mistakes you can make
in writing your will,
fifty ways to improve your memory,
and promotions to buy old movies
whose actors have long been dead.

You realize your age when
the pledge drives on public television
for weeks without stopping
are concerts of has-been hippies,
those now left standing.

Magazines invite you to spend your last days
riding trikes in carefree retirement communities
or holding miniature dogs in your laps
with folks who are white-haired, smiling,
and incredibly youthful.

Your friends send letters from Florida
and one of them used to be
your student teacher.
You fall asleep during news of drugs and terrorists
but you lock your doors on Sunday mornings.

And you know you're really getting up there when
the first pages you read in the newspapers
are the obituaries
and, happily, this time,
you don't recognize any names.

Safekeeping

An old aunt cherished a silver tea set.
She polished it up and stashed it away
in the back of the darkened cupboard
hidden from possible thieves.
It never gleamed in sunlight
or sparkled its beauty to friends.

My neighbor labored over a cutting garden
a rainbow of zinnias, snapdragons, and phlox.
No family or friend was permitted to cut them
they never traveled indoors to her table.
They had to remain outdoors where she nursed them,
no first-hand aroma filled the home.

A lady in water aerobics class
hoarded a star-studded amethyst swimsuit.
Saved for a trip to the beach someday,
it lingered ten years in the bottom drawer.
Protected from chemicals in the pool,
it never drowned or came up for air.

For years I've wanted to tell them all:
Drink from cobalt Venetian goblets,
pour tea into delicate Wedgewood cups,
slip the heirloom onto your finger.
Now that your lives are nearly done,
why are you burying all your treasures?

Colors Before Dark

October always flashes brilliant colors—
Maple leaves turn bloody red,
flutter down to browning grass
always, always before November gloom.
And the sky turns violent tangerine,
sun drops apologetically
behind the harbor
into the deep shadows across the bay.
Also the embers in the dying fire
snap into blinding gold
within the glowing woodstove
before they turn to final gray.
All things glow bright and brilliant
before they slide into black.
What joy to see the colors
once again
before the final dark.

Adrift in the Grass

Whatever happened to the red snowmobile
swallowed up by grass in the greening field
sad and alone
out of place
in a strange setting?

Who abandoned it when snow was gone?
Were there hopes for its adoption?
The whole summer passed
weeds emerged and spat out seeds
around its red shiny metal.

Yesterday it disappeared
and in its resting place
of waving grass
was a broken down wooden boat
languishing in the pasture.

I wonder how many of us
will end our days like this
confused and bewildered
out of place
adrift in a sea of grass.

Minstrel

He wakes, perspiring, from a dream,
stretched out at back of lurching bus,
his guitar pressed against his chest.
His fingers linger on the frets,
desperate to continue, but
scraps and bills spread out beside him.
No time to make the music,
no space to pull the lyrics
from the clutter in his mind.
The traveling minstrel scribbles
words on shreds of paper napkins,
snatching minutes on the road,
mindful of the passing hours.
Evening glow will soon be gone.
He hopes, before the dark will rise,
there might be time for one more song.

Footsteps in the Night

Before dawn I listen
to cats' paws
treading on papers
or blankets.
In the dark of the quiet house
soft pads creep
on quilts, books,
tabletops, slipcovers,
feather beds and counter tops.
Half awake, I dream
that I am walking past a wooded lot.
Heavy feet are crunching through leafy paths.
Maybe I should stop to greet the traveler
but hair on my neck rises up to warn me
of danger, to be wary
of someone who could harm me.
Are there footsteps
coming to claim me?
Is it finally time
for me to go?

How We Leave

My young son gazes down
from his frame on the bedroom wall
pensive in his graduation portrait.
He smashed out of this world
in a crash of fire and twisted steel.
But I will crawl out
on my hands and knees.

The Forest Circle

The great blue heron lifts and circles round
the creeping trail that hugs the riverside.
The crunch of footfalls are the only sounds
to stir the timid animals that hide

where hardwoods grow and stretch up to the sky,
centurions of the forest in their prime
until they age, host lichen, rot and die,
give life to insects, fungi, birds that climb

and scatter seeds that under snow are hidden.
The seedlings rise to life in vernal sun,
emerging through the squirrels' middens.
The forest's endless web of life is spun:

an amazing, perfect, timeless circle,
nature's true enduring miracle.

Sarah Jane (aka Sally) Woolf-Wade has studied the craft of poetry with John Holmes, Judith Steinbergh, Wes McNair, Billy Collins, Sam Hammill, Betsy Sholl, Baron Wormser, Martin Steingesser, Tom Lux, Laure-Anne Bosselaar, and other poets. Most of her adult life has been spent as a teacher, and many summers as mate on a windjammer, sailing daytrippers around the Boston Harbor islands.

Her poems have appeared in *Northern New England Review*, the *Mid-American Poetry Review*, *Off the Coast*, *The Maine Poetry Review*, *Puckerbrush Review*, *Goose River Anthology*, *Robert Frost Anthology*, Wes McNair's "Take Heart" series, *Port City Poems*, and other Maine presses. She has participated in local readings including CONA's "Peaceful Beginnings," Gordon Bok's "Working on the Water" programs, Wes McNair's "Maine Poetry Express," the 200th Anniversary of the Battle between the *U.S.S. Enterprise* and the *H.M.S. Boxer* at Pemaquid Point, and Maine Maritime Museum's "Voices of the Sea." The Maine Poets Society awarded her second prize in 2013 for "No Man's Land" and first prize in 2014 for "Northhaven Autumn." Three collections of poetry include *Tidepools, Nightsong, Down the Bristol Road*, and a book of historical fiction for young readers, *Downwind from Pemaquid*, which won Honorable Mention at the New England Book Festival. She is associated with the former Pemaquid Poets Group and the current Maine Poets Society. She lives with her husband in New Harbor, Maine.

www.ingramcontent.com/pod-product-compliance
Lightning Source LLC
Chambersburg PA
CBHW030526080526
44586CB00011B/340